Prospectus of The Complete Works of Abraham Lincoln

Comprising his Speeches, Letters, State Papers and Miscellaneous Writings

JOHN G. NICOLAY AND JOHN HAY

Published by Left of Brain Books

Copyright © 2021 Left of Brain Books

ISBN 978-1-396-32154-2

First Edition

All rights reserved. No part of this publication may be reproduced, distributed, or transmitted in any form or by any means, including photocopying, recording, or other electronic or mechanical methods, without the prior written permission of the publisher, except in the case of brief quotations embodied in critical reviews and certain other noncommercial uses permitted by copyright law. Left of Brain Books is a division of Left of Brain Onboarding Pty Ltd.

Table of Contents

A Word from President Roosevelt 1
The Work of Nicolay & Hay 2
New Material 3
Arrangement 3
Notes 4
Special Articles 4
Bibliography 5
Index 5
Mechanical Construction 6
Paper 6
Type 7
Illustrations 7
Binding 8
Authority for Publication 9
Introductions 10
Some of the Important Additions to the First Edition 11
Illustrations 12
Estimates of Lincoln's Literary Ability 13
Opinions of the First Edition 15
A Letter from a Celebrated American Historian 16
A Few of Lincoln's Epigrams 18
Some Topics of Present Vital Interest of
Which Lincoln Wrote 19

A Word from President Roosevelt

"I FEEL that not merely all lovers of the Republican party but all believers in the country should do everything in their power to keep alive the memory of Abraham Lincoln. The problems we have to solve as a nation now are not the same as those he had to face; but they can be solved aright only if we bring to the solution exactly his principles and his methods, his iron resolution, his keen good sense, his broad kindliness, his practical ability, and his lofty idealism.

"Faithfully yours,
"THEODORE ROOSEVELT."

LETTER TO THE REPUBLICAN CLUB,
NEW YORK, JANUARY 26, 1903.

The Work of Nicolay & Hay

THE edition of Abraham Lincoln's Works collected by Mr. John G. Nicolay and Col. John Hay must ever be regarded by students as the only complete, the only authorized, and the only standard collection.

For nearly thirty years they labored on this monumental work, and their positions as his Private Secretaries during the whole period of Lincoln's official life, gave them opportunities which were beyond the reach of all others. One of them, and generally both, were on duty at Mr. Lincoln's side every day through the pregnant years from 1860 to 1865. During all this time they collected material from day to-day for this work, and the President himself encouraged and assisted them. SOME OF HIS MOST PRECIOUS MANUSCRIPTS WERE GIVEN TO THEM BY HIS OWN HANDS.

For twenty years after President Lincoln's death they gave most of their time to the collection and arrangement of the enormous amount of material at their disposal. The succeeding Secretaries of War gave them free and constant access to the official records, and Col. Robert T. Lincoln—the only surviving member of the President's family—turned over to them all his father's papers. This added a vast amount of private material which had not come within the sphere of their official knowledge, and added the charming personal element to the works of the great statesman. When Colonel Lincoln requested them to compile his father's writings and freely transferred to them all his legal rights as his father's heir to protection by copyright, he at once made their collection the standard edition for all time, and rendered it impossible for any unauthorized publisher to successfully compete with them by issuing any edition which could have even the semblance of being complete.

New Material

THE eleven years which have elapsed since the first edition of this work was issued have but served to augment the honor, esteem, and love in which the people of America have ever held the Great War President. Naturally this national attitude has resulted in bringing to light a large amount of manuscript material—much of great historical and biographical value—which inevitably escaped even such conscientious workers as Mr. Nicolay and Colonel Hay. It required the work of numerous collectors in widely scattered places and the inevitable winnowing of time to bring these various items to light. Now, however, the field has been well worked. Few, if any, items of importance can be any longer hidden. This, therefore, seems to be the appropriate time to gather and add them to the work of the original editors, which is thus rounded out and made a complete and definitive collection. No attempt has been made to include every scrap of Lincoln's writings, such as mere memoranda of unimportant happenings, nor brief notes to unknown persons. The aim has been to include everything which could throw light upon the marvellously varied characteristics of the man, or tend to elucidate the terribly complex historical, political, and social conditions amid which he lived. As nearly twenty per cent. more of Lincoln's own writings, culled from numerous public and private collections, have been added to the first edition, it may safely be said that this result has been achieved.

Arrangement

AFTER long consideration the editors decided upon a strictly chronological arrangement. In no other way could the many-sidedness of Lincoln be so clearly displayed, nor the relation of events be so vividly shown. The lovableness of Lincoln, the man, is apparent when, in the midst of the Lincoln and Douglas debates, he finds time to write a note guaranteeing the credit of a poor friend for furniture, or when, amidst the stirring times of 1864 and the pressing cares State imposed upon him, his fine sympathy bursts eloquently forth in the celebrated letter to Mrs. Bixby. By such an arrangement of his writings, Lincoln is shown to the world as he was from day to day. Instead of being merely a valuable collection of raw material for the future historian, arranged by some hard and fast system, it becomes a true history of himself and his times as written, not alone in his own words, but by his own actions—a human document pulsating with the life and the love, the greatness and the generosity, the sympathy and the shrewdness of one of the most illustrious men who ever lived.

Notes

IN ORDER that the work may be read intelligently, without unduly taxing the reader's memory or involving him in laborious research, notes have been added to the text where they were deemed necessary to remind the reader of the events which inspired the author's words, to explain obscure allusions, or to preserve the continuity of the narrative. The aim has been to make these notes as few and as brief as is compatible with a clear understanding of the subject.

Special Articles

NEARLY every eminent man has been inspired by Lincoln's marvelous personality to deliver some tribute to his genius. Some of these were published in pamphlets which have long been out of print, others are buried in forgotten newspapers, while others again are only found among the author's works in connection with unrelated essays, etc. In order to preserve the most important of these in permanent form, they have been printed as Special Introductions to the various volumes. They show the estimates of Lincoln's greatness by eminent men who were his contemporaries, but whose points of view were as varied as their own personalities, and, taken together, they form a many-sided, many-minded biography.

Bibliography

THE SAME causes which have hitherto made it impossible to issue a complete edition of Lincoln's works have made it equally impossible to compile a complete bibliography. Many attempts to do this have been made, and each one has shown careful and diligent research and has prepared the way for others still more complete. The bibliography which appears in the last volume of this set results from a careful comparison and consolidation of previous bibliographies, numerous large public library and trade catalogues, and is supplemented by all the latest accessions to the libraries of a number of famous private collectors. It is impossible to assure completeness in a matter of this kind, but at least this bibliography will mark one more step in that direction and contain all the information upon the subject which is at present available.

Index

THE WHOLE work, including the special articles, will be fully indexed. In short, no expense will be spared, no effort will be saved which could help to make this the most valuable contribution to the Literature of Lincoln.

Mechanical Construction

HARMONY is the great essential of art. As discords offend the ear or incongruous colors hurt the eye, so a book, which is dressed in a mechanical garb unsuited to its subject matter, insults the tastes of the true book-lover. The mechanical features of this work have been designed to reflect something of the characteristics of the illustrious author. The rugged grandeur, the simple forcefulness, the lovable character, and the old time honesty of Lincoln find their prototypes in the quiet dignity, the severe simplicity, the old time beauty, and the honest execution of the mechanical details. No fanciful ornamentation, no smug conventionality have been attempted. Just the most readable type, the most perfect workmanship, the very best materials, the most simple designs, executed after the plans of the old masters of printing and binding, have been combined to make a truly harmonious, and hence beautiful, result.

Paper

THE life of a book is in the paper upon which it is printed, and the life of the paper depends principally upon the amount of rag stock used in its composition. In its report upon paper, The Royal Society of Arts says: "The practical evidence as to permanence fully confirms this classification ... and that the paper-making fibres may be ranged in four classes.

"A. Cotton, flax, and hemp.
"Wood cellulose.
"C. Esparto and straw cellulose.
"D. Mechanical wood pulp.
"In regard, therefore, to papers for books and documents of permanent value, the selection must be taken in this order."

The paper upon which this edition is printed is made entirely of rag stock. It is manufactured especially for this work by The Riverside Paper Mills, one of the oldest and most reliable mills in America, having been in business for over a hundred years. This paper is the culminating masterpiece of their vast experience. As such, it has been called Riverside, after their mills. Every sheet made for this edition is water-marked with a fac-simile of President Lincoln's autograph. It is a pure white, deckle-edge, antique, wove paper of beautiful texture, weight and finish. It is especially manufactured with the idea of developing to the utmost all the beauties of the type, and of supplying to the binder the best possible foundation for his art. Its durability, firmness and flexibility, added to its other qualifications, make it the book paper *par excellence*.

Type

THE celebrated Pica Caslon type has been selected on account of its great legibility, the chaste beauty of its letters, and the peculiarly harmonious relation it bears to the antique paper used. This type was cut by William Caslon in London early in the eighteenth century. It has ever since been regarded by connoisseurs as one of the most beautiful and readable designs ever cut. Other type founders strove to rival, and some to imitate, its beauties with varying degrees of success, until a few years ago not only the original matrices, but even the original steel type from which the matrices were made, cut by the hand of William Caslon himself, were discovered in his old printing-shop. To secure a perfect impression from the type a special grade of ink has been used and every precaution taken to insure an even distribution and a perfect register.

Illustrations

THE illustrations found in this edition, of which there are approximately one hundred in all, would by themselves make it a valuable addition to any collection of Lincolniana. All the famous portraits of Lincoln are reproduced, together with many that are very rare—

some of them being known to but few collectors. Portraits of the leading generals of the Civil War, members of Lincoln's Cabinet, etc., add completeness and variety to the collection. Such illustrations taken from authentic sources really illuminate the text, as well as add to the artistic beauty of the book. Each illustration is reproduced by the process best suited to bring out its full value, whether in photogravure, wood cut, copper line engraving, or photographic processes. Important letters and documents are given in fac-simile from almost priceless originals in Lincoln's own handwriting.

Binding

THE bindings of the volumes are in keeping with the excellence of the other mechanical features. Especial pains have been taken with the sewing and forwarding to make the book flexible and durable. The designs of the tooling are chaste and dignified, but the care with which they have been executed and the high quality of the materials used, combine to make the result as rich and beautiful as it is simple and unobtrusive.

Authority for Publication

"MAY 30, 1893.

"*My Dear Nicolay*: As you and Colonel Hay have now brought your great work to a most successful conclusion by the publication of your life of my father, I hope and request that you and he will supplement it by collecting, editing, and publishing the speeches, letters, state papers, and miscellaneous writings of my father. You and Colonel Hay have my consent and authority to obtain for yourselves such protection by copyright, or otherwise, in respect to the whole or any part of such a collection, as I might for any reason be entitled to have.

"Believe me very sincerely yours,
"ROBERT T. LINCOLN."

"JOHN G. NICOLAY."

Both in fulfilment of the request contained in foregoing letter, and in execution of a long-cherished design, we present to the public this edition of the "Complete Works of Abraham Lincoln," hoping and trusting that it will be received as a welcome addition to American historical literature.

JOHN G. NICOLAY.
JOHN HAY.

Introductions

Richard Watson Gilder: "Lincoln as a Writer."

Horace Greeley: "An Estimate of the Career of Abraham Lincoln."

Charles Sumner: "Abraham Lincoln and the Promises of the Declaration of Independence."

Phillips Brooks: "The Life and Character of Abraham Lincoln."

Robert Ingersoll: "The Influence of Abraham Lincoln."

George Bancroft: "The Life and Character of Abraham Lincoln."

William McKinley: "Abraham Lincoln, the Great Republican."

James Abram Garfield: "Lincoln and Emancipation."

Henry Ward Beecher: "The Loss of Lincoln."

Frank S. Black: "The Greatness of Lincoln."

Some of the Important Additions to the First Edition

The Rebecca Letters Leading up to the Duel with Shields.

Some of Lincoln's Early Poems.

Report of Lincoln's Campaign in Massachusetts.

Two Speeches of Douglas preliminary to the Debates proper.

A large number of Important Letters to Statesmen and Generals, and other material.

Hundreds of personal letters heretofore unpublished in any edition of Lincoln's writings.

Official letters to Seward and fellow members of the Cabinet.

Notable letter to Major-General Hunter.

A great number of telegrams during the Civil War period that prove "Lincoln was his best General."

Early law arguments.

Important speech before the Illinois Legislature in 1837.

Legal opinions.

Speech to the 12th Indiana Regiment.

New letters to Generals Halleck, McClellan, and Meade.

Illustrations

AMONG THE ILLUSTRATIONS ARE REPRODUCTIONS OF THE FOLLOWING:

The Carpenter Portrait.

Several of the Thomas Johnson Engravings.

Several Photographs by Brady.

Several Engravings by Sartain.

Lincoln's Last Photograph.

Group Picture of Lincoln, Nicolay, and Hay, with a letter from the latter explaining it.

Log Cabin built by Lincoln.

Lincoln Statue in Florence, Italy.

The Saint-Gauden Monument.

Portraits of Members of Lincoln's Cabinet.

Portraits of the Generals of the Civil War.

A Number of Rare Portraits never before published in any book.

FACSIMILES OF

Gettysburg Address—the First Draft and the Final Revision.

The Famous Letter to Mrs. Bixby.

Letter to the General Conference of the Methodist Episcopal Church.

The Emancipation Proclamation.

And many other important documents.

Estimates of Lincoln's Literary Ability

"He would doubtless have been very much surprised if any one had told him that he had a 'style' at all, and yet, because he was determined to be understood, ... he achieved a singularly clear and forcible style, which took color from his own noble character, and became a thing individual and distinguished."—Richard Watson Gilder.

"His rejection of what is called fine writing was as deliberate as St. Paul's, and for the same reason—because he felt that he was speaking on a subject which must be made clear to the lowest intellect, though it should fail to captivate the highest. But we say of Lincoln's writings ... They are brief, condensed, intense, and with a power of insight and expression which makes them worthy to be inscribed in letters of gold."—Harriet Beecher Stowe.

"Probably there are few finer passages in literature than the close of Lincoln's inaugural address."—Robert G. Ingersoll.

"His style was his own, formed on no model, and springing directly from himself. ... There are passages which will live always. It is no exaggeration to say that, in weight and pith, suffused in a certain practical color, they call to mind Bacon's essays. Such passages make an epoch in State papers."—Charles Sumner.

"This (second inaugural) was like a sacred poem. No American President has ever spoken words like these to the American people. America never had a President who found such words in the depth of his heart."—Carl Schurz.

"The weight and penetration of many passages in his letters, messages, and speeches ... what pregnant definitions; what unerring common sense; what foresight; and, on great occasions, what lofty, and more than national, what humane tone! His brief speech at Gettysburg will not easily be surpassed by words on any recorded occasion."—Ralph Waldo Emerson.

"Lincoln had a style—a distinctive, individual, characteristic form of expression. In his own way he gained an insight into the structure of English, and a freedom and skill in the selection of and combination of words, which not only made him the most convincing speaker of his time, but which have secured for his speeches a permanent place in literature."—Hamilton Wright Mabie.

"Each of Lincoln's paragraphs is an organism. Each is knit together by perfect logical sequence, perfect unity. ... The letter is a challenge. Each sentence is meant to go home like a shot."—Edwin Herbert Lewis.

"Perhaps no point in the career of Abraham Lincoln has excited more surprise or comment than his remarkable power of literary expression. It is a constant puzzle to many men of letters how a person growing up without advantages of schools and books could have acquired the art which enabled him to write the Gettysburg Address and the Second Inaugural."—John G. Nicolay.

"The second of the American statesmen holding high rank as a man of letters was Abraham Lincoln, whose later State Papers are models not only in insight and in tact, but in expression also."—Brander Matthews.

"It is just appreciation, not extravagance, to say that the ... volume containing the Lincoln and Douglas debates holds some of the masterpieces of oratory of all ages and nations."—John T. Morse, Jr.

Opinions of the First Edition

THE editors of these works have shown great diligence in collecting material from the date of the first document, March 9, 1832, down to the end. The order of arrangement is chronological. ... The "works" are indispensable to all students of our later political history.—*Literature of American History.* Issued by authority of The American Library Association.

The editors of "Abraham Lincoln's Complete Works" have prepared them on the same grand scale as their "Life of Lincoln." ... These works will be sure to find their way into all libraries, public and private, the owners or managers of which make any pretension to keeping abreast of the political history of the country.—Professor B. A. Hinsdale, of Ann Arbor University, *The Dial,* July 16, 1894.

The materials are arranged in chronological order, and as they include an autobiography composed by Lincoln himself in 1860, after his nomination for the presidency, it is possible for the careful reader of these volumes to obtain a correct general idea of Lincoln's principles and achievements without recourse to any other work.—New York *Sun,* May 20, 1894.

As a work of reference in relation to the political and military history of the Civil War this collection of Lincoln's writings at once takes its place in every American library of any pretensions, and it will never be supplanted. To read these pages is not only to revive memories of the heroic period of arms, but also to gain an appreciative idea of the inexhaustible resources of patience, sagacity, industry, and courage displayed by the martyr leader of the nation.—New York *Tribune,* June 24, 1894.

A Letter from a Celebrated American Historian

(*From The Century Magazine*)

During the academic year 1894-95, at the University of Pennsylvania, perhaps for the first time in this country, the "Speeches, State Papers, and Miscellaneous Writings" of Abraham Lincoln were made the basis of a special course for graduate students in the constitutional history of this country, from the repeal of the Missouri Compromise in 1850 to the adoption of the Fifteenth Amendment to the Constitution in 1870. Of the course of American government, commonwealth and national, during this period, relatively far less is known than of its course during the entire preceding period of our history. Nor is this strange. The political ideas of our earlier statesmen, Washington, Franklin, Adams, Jefferson, Hamilton, Marshall, and of their immediate successors, Webster, Calhoun, Clay, Benton, have been accessible in their published works. But of the ideas of the succeeding generation of our public men but little is now known. After 1850 the histories of the United States become military records: the evolution of American government is imperfectly traced in the best of them. Military history has little place in a course of study outside of a military school. There is not at present a constitutional history of the United States during the most critical period of our history—from 1850 to the close of the era of reconstruction. There is, however, a vast mass of material comprising the documentary record of American government, commonwealth and national, during this period in the various departments—legislative, judicial, executive, and administrative.

This material, comprising about thirty thousand volumes, has never been collected in one library, and it is impossible for any other than the wealthiest universities to possess even a portion of it. Most American schools, in the courses in American history and government which they offer, must be satisfied to use the works of American statesmen and the treatises prepared by specialists.

During this critical period of our nineteenth Century history, Abraham Lincoln bears a part and serves a function comparable only to Washington's in the eighteenth century.

The publication of the "Complete Works of Lincoln" by The Century Company in 1894 is the most important contribution of our times to a just conception of the evolution of American democracy during this period. In the debates with Senator Douglas, Lincoln is the voice of American democracy. He is not then the Lincoln whom we now know; he is the Lincoln of political debate, not the Lincoln of national administration. He grew in thought as the people grew. In his State papers this growth is recorded; and it is undoubtedly true that in no other records of the time is the course of public opinion in America so accurately traced as in the speeches, in the state papers, and in the miscellaneous writings of this man.

His political ideas are, in our day at least, authoritative and classic, and the exhaustive study of them is the natural course for any person who expects to understand the political evolution since his death.

Aside from the fascinating character of the man himself, the study of his notions of representative government, in correlation with the course of events in which his was individually the leading mind, is an equipment for American citizenship; and such equipment was never more needed than at the present time.

FRANCIS N. THORPE.

UNIVERSITY OF PENNSYLVANIA

A Few of Lincoln's Epigrams

"LET us have faith that right makes might, and in that faith let us, to the end, dare to do our duty as we understand it."

"In law it is good policy never to plead what you need not, lest you oblige yourself to prove what you cannot."

"By a course of reasoning, Euclid proves that all the angles in a triangle are equal to two right angles. Now, if you undertake to disprove that proposition, would you prove it false by calling Euclid a liar?"

"Human action can be modified to some extent, but human nature cannot be changed."

"We shall sooner have a fowl by hatching the egg than by smashing it."

"There is no grievance that is a fit object of redress by mob law."

"No man is good enough to govern another man without that other's consent."

"War does not admit of holidays."

Some Topics of Present Vital Interest of Which Lincoln Wrote

ACQUISITION of Territory — Acts of Incorporation — Admission of States into Union — Agriculture — Aliens — American Industries — Amnesty — Anarchy — Appropriations — Arbitration — Army and Army Organization — Articles of Confederation — Asiatic Trade — Assassination — Atlantic Cable.

BALLOT, Power of — Bank Charters and Circulation — Bankrupt Law — Behring Straits — Bible Texts — Borrowed Money — British North America Boundary.

CANADIAN Commerce — Canals — Capital and Labor — Capital Punishment — Cavalry — Census — Children and Laws — China — Citizenship — Civil and Religious Liberty — Coast Guard — Colonization of Negroes — Commerce (Domestic and Foreign) — Constitution (U. S.) — Consular System — Contraband of War — Contracts — Cotton Culture and Manufacture — Cuban Annexation — Currency.

DEBT — Declaration of Independence — Democratic Party — Dictatorship — Diplomatic Corps — Disunion — Domestic Policy — Draft Law — Drama — Dred Scott Decision.

ECONOMY — Education — Election Laws — Electoral College — Emancipation — Employment — Enlistment — Equality — European Policy — Evasion of Laws — Executions.

FARMERS — Federal Government — Finance — Fisheries — Foreign Intervention — Foreign Arbitration — Foreign Policy — Forfeitures — Fortification (coast) — Fractional Currency — Fraternities — Free Democracy — Freedom of the Press — Free Institutions — Free Labor Systems — Free Trade — Fusion Views.

GENERAL Government (principles) — General Land Office — Gold Mines — Government Lands — Great Lakes — Guerrilla Warfare — Gulf Ports — Gunboats and Guns.

HABEAS Corpus — Hanseatic Republics — Harbors — Harvesting Methods — Hayti, Relations with — Highway Improvement — Homestead Law — Hotchkiss Projectiles — Human Nature.

ILLICIT Trade — Immigration — Imports — Indemnity — Indian Affairs — Industrial Classes — Infantry — Insurrection — Intemperance — Internal Improvements — Internal Revenue Act — Ironclads.

JAPAN (trade) — Jews — Judicial System — Juries — Jurisdiction.

LABOR — Land Appropriation — Law Study — Law of Nations — Legal Tender — Legislation — Letters of Marque — Liberty — Liquor Traffic — Loans (Government) — Luxuries (taxation of) — Lynch Law.

MANUFACTURES — Maritime Nations — Martial Law — Matrimony — Mechanics — Militia and Military affairs — Mineral Resources — Mining — Mints — Miscegenation — Mob Law — Monarchy — Money — Monroe Doctrine — Moral Reforms.

NATIONAL Banks — National Debt — National Loans — Naturalization Laws — Navy and Naval Affairs — Negroes — Neutral Rights — Newspapers — Nicaragua — Nullification.

OATHS — Office — seeking — Oligarchy — Ordinances — Ordnance.

PARDONS — Party Platforms — Patents — Patriotism — Patronage — Pay — system — Pensions — Phonetics — Plantation Cultivation — Platforms, National — Poetry — Police Regulation — Polygamy Question — Popular Sovereignty — Postal Affairs — Precedents — Presidency — Printing — Prisons — Protection — Public Debt — Public Improvements — Public Lands — Public Schools — Punishment and Crime.

RACE Prejudice — Railroad Corporations — Railroad Systems — Reciprocity — Reconstruction — Religion — Representative Government — Republicanism — Revenue — Rights of the People — River and Harbor Improvements — Roads, Construction — Russian Relations.

SANITARY Commissions — Science — Seacoast Fortification — Secret Societies — Sectionalism — Sedition Law — Self — government — Shipyards — Slavery — Specie Squatter Sovereignty — Standing Army — State Banks — State Rights — Suffrage.

TARIFF — Taxation — Telegraphs — Temperance — Territories — Title to Soil — Treason — Treaties — Trial by Jury.

UNION (State) — U. S. Army — U. S. Bank — U. S. Constitution — U. S. Government — U. S. Mail — U. S. Navy — Usury.

VETO Power — Volunteers.

WARS — Woman Suffrage — Workingmen.

www.ingramcontent.com/pod-product-compliance
Lightning Source LLC
Chambersburg PA
CBHW020830020526
44118CB00032B/546